The BARGE Book

JERRY BUSHEY

CAROLRHODA BOOKS · MINNEAPOLIS

*The author would like to extend
special thanks to Cargo Carriers Inc.,
Jerry Brown, John D. Franklin, the crew
of the Badger, and Capital Barge for
their good-spirited help in making
this book possible.*

*Photos on pages, 5, 29, 30, and 31
courtesy of Cargo Carriers Inc.*

LIBRARY OF CONGRESS CATALOGING IN PUBLICATION DATA

Bushey, Jerry.
The barge book.

Summary: Text and photographs describe the progres-
sion of cargo barges down the Mississippi River from
Minneapolis to New Orleans.
1. Inland water transportation–Mississippi River–
Juvenile literature. 2. Barges–Mississippi River–
Juvenile literature. 3. Towboats–Mississippi River–
Juvenile literature. 4. River boats–Mississippi
River–Juvenile literature. [1. Barges. 2. Inland
water transportation–Mississippi River] I. Title.
HE630.M6B87 1984   386'.354'0977 83-7746
ISBN 0-87614-205-6 (lib. bdg.)

1 2 3 4 5 6 7 8 9 10 90 89 88 87 86 85 84

To my wife and best friend, Elaine

Q. What is 195 feet long, 35 feet wide, and carries as much cargo as 15 railroad cars or 65 semi trucks?

A. *One River Barge*

Barges have been around for thousands and thousands of years. They were traveling up and down the Nile River when the Egyptians were building the pyramids, and they probably date back even further than that. The very first barges were simple rafts that people pushed along with poles. Later barges had oars or sails. Today's river barges are pushed by powerful boats called towboats, but they are still used for the same reason barges were used thousands of years ago—to carry heavy loads from one place to another.

River barge shipping is very important in the United States, and one of the most important barging rivers is the "Mighty Mississippi." Barges travel on the Mississippi all the way from Minneapolis/St. Paul, Minnesota, to New Orleans, Louisiana, a distance of 1,837 miles!

The trip is divided into two parts. The first part is from Minneapolis to St. Louis, Missouri, a distance of 669 miles. The water level on this part of the river, called the *upper river*, is uneven, so a series of locks and dams has been built to help barges and other boats travel on it. Where the water is too shallow for boats, dams make it deeper by holding back the water upstream. Locks are huge channels through the dams. They operate a little like elevators to carry boats from one side of a dam to the other.

The second part of the trip is from St. Louis to New Orleans, a distance of 1,168 miles. This part of the river, called the *lower river*, is wide and deep, so there is no need for locks and dams.

CANADA

Lake Itasca

MINNESOTA

LAKE SUPERIOR

Minneapolis ● ● St. Paul

WISCONSIN

LAKE MICHIGAN

IOWA

Dubuque

Davenport

ILLINOIS

Hannibal

MISSOURI

St. Louis ●

Cairo

KENTUCKY

TENNESSEE

ARKANSAS

● Memphis

MISSISSIPPI

LOUISIANA

● Vicksburg

● Baton Rouge

Mississippi Delta

GULF OF MEXICO

THE MISSISSIPPI RIVER
Lock and Dam — ⌇

There are many places in the Minneapolis/St. Paul area where barges are loaded with grain, iron, petroleum, coal, vegetable oil, sulphur, and machinery. This grain-loading facility is just one of them. Each year 1½ billion bushels of grain are shipped downriver. Three-fourths of the grain shipped out of the midwest and two-thirds of the grain exported from the United States travels down the Mississippi by barge before going on to its final destination.

Corn is being loaded into this barge—52,000 bushels of it weighing about 2 million pounds. Two million pounds of cargo will make 9 feet of the barge ride below the surface of the water. Most barges carry this much weight when the depth of the upper river is normal. Then the shipping channel is at least 10 feet deep. When there is a dry spell and the river is shallower, the barges must carry less weight.

Barges make their journey down the Mississippi tied together in groups called *tows.* When a barge has been filled, it is moved to a place where it is joined with other barges. The barge is taken to this location by a small towboat called a *dinner-bucket boat.* The name comes from the fact that there are no kitchens (called *galleys* on a boat) on these small towboats, so the crew members must bring their meals on board with them. In times past they carried their meals in dinner buckets.

The barge in the background of the photograph was loaded in Minneapolis and is on its way downriver to meet other barges in St. Paul. In order to get from Minneapolis to St. Paul, it must pass through the first lock on its journey. This is the lock and dam at the Falls of St. Anthony.

The St. Anthony Falls lock and dam was built by the U.S. Army Corps of Engineers in the early 1900s. Before that time the river above the dam was too shallow for large boats. The dam makes the river deeper by holding back the water upstream. Boats pass through the dam by way of the lock.

Every lock has two gates—one on the upstream end and one on the downstream end. When a barge is traveling downstream, like this one, it enters the lock through the upstream gate.

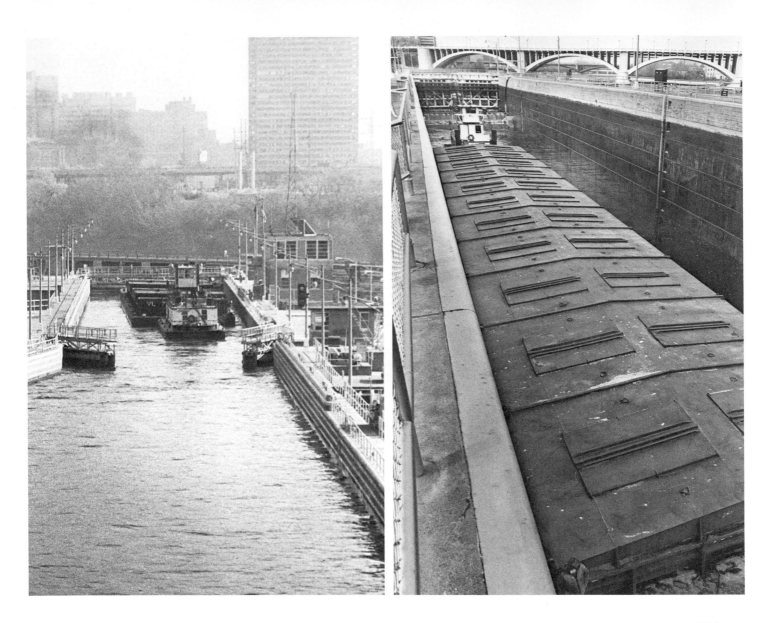

Once it is safely inside the lock, the gate closes. Valves in the floor of the lock are then opened and the water drains out of the lock until it is at the same level as the water on the downstream side of the dam.

Then the lock's downstream gate is opened, and the barge
leaves the lock and continues on its way.

These barges are being tied together into a tow. A dinner-bucket boat assembles the barges.

When the barge arrives in St. Paul, it is tied together with other barges into a tow. Barges always travel down the river in tows. Whatever the number of barges being pushed, they must be tied together very tightly with steel cable. The tow must be like one big unit so that it can be steered. The barges are assembled with the help of the dinner-bucket boats. It can take anywhere from two hours to four days to assemble a tow.

Meanwhile, the large towboat that will push the tow from
St. Paul to St. Louis is waiting to get underway.

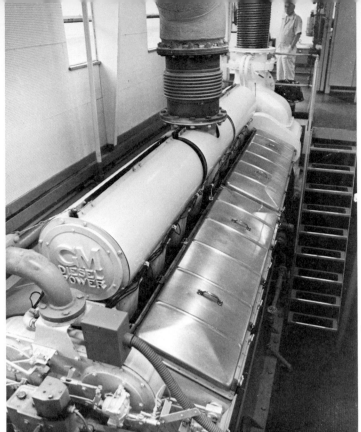

Facing page: This control panel in the engine room tells the engineer how the engines and all the other mechanical systems on the boat are functioning.

The chief engineer checks one of the towboat's two engines.

Before the towboat begins the trip downriver, the chief engineer checks to see that its engines are working properly. The engines are not turned off when the boat is docked. In fact, unless something goes wrong, the engines will run for the entire shipping season—about eight months—without ever being shut off!

This towboat has two very powerful engines. Together they use about 2,400 gallons of fuel per day. That is a lot of fuel, but barges can move 1 ton of cargo 500 miles on a single gallon of the towboat's fuel. A semi truck can move 1 ton of cargo only 60 miles on a gallon of fuel. This fuel efficiency is one reason why barge shipping is so common.

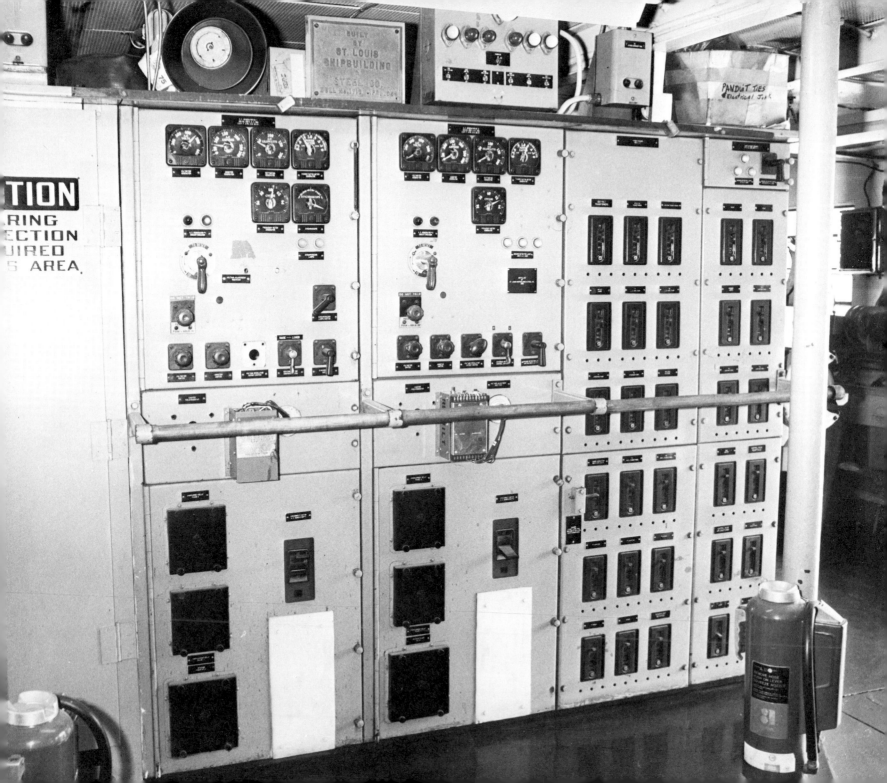

The chief engineer fixes a light.

Two crew members eat before going on duty.

This towboat has a crew of 12 people. There are always 6 people on duty at a time, including either the captain, who is the person in charge, or the pilot, who helps steer the towboat. Crew members work 6-hour shifts (6 hours on duty, then 6 hours off) for 30 days in a row. Then they get 30 days off. Even though they work only about 6 months a year, towboat crew members often work 200 hours more each year than people with regular jobs.

Right: Deckhand's sleeping quarters

Below: The captain's and pilot's lounge

Above: Captain's sleeping quarters

Left: The cook is busy preparing a meal in the galley.

When the tow has been assembled, the captain takes the towboat to where it is docked and waiting. This towboat is starting its journey with only a 6-barge tow, but as it travels down the river it will pick up more barges until it has a full tow of 15.

As the tow starts out, we can look over the pilot's shoulder and see one of the many bridges under which it must pass. Steering underneath bridges can be tricky, especially in a case like this where there are two bridges in a row. The tow must come out from under the first bridge in exactly the right position to go under the next one. It takes more than half a mile to stop a tow, so if it isn't in the right position, it could hit the second bridge before the pilot would be able to stop it.

Horst, the pilot, looks pretty unconcerned as he steers the tow under the bridges, but he takes his work very seriously. It took him 12 years to become a pilot. Barge companies must be able to trust their pilots and captains completely. They are piloting 2- to 3-million-dollar boats pushing 5 million dollars worth of cargo! Before a person can become an upper river pilot, he or she must know all 669 miles of the upper river by memory. This isn't easy because the river is always changing.

There are 27 locks and dams between St. Paul and St. Louis plus 2 more in Minneapolis/St. Paul. Because of the size of the locks, tows on the upper river cannot contain more than 15 barges. Only 9 barges can go through the lock at one time, so a full tow must go through in shifts. First 9 barges go through, then 6 more barges and the towboat. This tow has only 6 barges, so the tow and towboat can go through together.

As the tow approaches the lock, the barges are in a straight line. The tow is going downstream, so it enters the upstream gate of the lock. Captain John D. carefully guides the barges into the lock. The front of the tow is about a city block away from the pilot house (a full tow of 15 is the length of 3 football fields), so the captain and the deckhand must talk to each other through microphones. The deckhand tells the captain how close the barges are to the walls of the lock.

Captain John D. carefully guides the barges into the lock.

The lock attendant walks beside the tow to the end of the lock.

A smaller boat is helping to guide this tow into the lock.

When the front of the tow gets into the lock, a deckhand throws a line that is tied to the tow to one of the lock attendants. The lock attendant walks beside the tow to the end of the lock. There he ties the line to the lock to keep the barges secure while the water level changes.

Sometimes the river current makes it difficult for a towboat to get a full tow into the locks. When this happens, the captain asks for help from a smaller boat. The smaller boat will guide the front of the tow into the lock.

Once the barges are in the lock, the towboat is unhooked from behind them, then hooked back up alongside them. When everything is ready, the gate is closed, the valves in the floor are opened, and the water level inside the lock begins to go down.

25

Finally the water in the lock is at the same level as the water on the downstream side of the gate. The downstream gate is then opened, and the barges are slowly pulled out with cables. The towboat is hooked up behind the barges again, and the trip downriver continues.

The tow will make stops along the way to pick up more barges until it has a full tow of 15. Then it will proceed to St. Louis. This trip usually takes from 4 to 5 days. From here to New Orleans the river is much wider and deeper. There are no more locks and dams, so more barges can now be added to the tow. Most of the barges that will be added are already assembled and waiting in St. Louis, although occasionally they are picked up somewhere along the way to New Orleans. As many as 30 barges might be added to a tow in St. Louis. A 45-barge tow carrying 50 million tons of cargo is a common sight on the lower river.

Since so many more barges have been added, a larger towboat must be used to push the tow from St. Louis to New Orleans. The towboat that brought the tow to St. Louis is now finished with this particular job. Its crew members will either take the towboat back to Minneapolis, where it will pick up another tow, or they will go home if their 30-day shift is over.

It is a smooth trip from St. Louis to New Orleans. The river is 20 to 30 feet deep in most places and up to a mile wide. The tow moves along at about 4 miles per hour, and the trip will take from 7 to 10 days. Unless barges are to be dropped off or picked up along the way, the tow will not stop again until it reaches New Orleans.

Finally the tow arrives in New Orleans. If the cargo is going to stay in the United States, it will probably be unloaded into a land-based station in the New Orleans area. Cargo is often unloaded with huge cranes or huge vacuums. The cargo can be stored for a time, or it may be transported by land to other parts of the U.S. right away.

If the cargo is going to be exported to other countries, the tow will probably travel farther south to the Gulf of Mexico. There the cargo can be unloaded directly into a ship.

Once the barges have been unloaded, their journey downriver is over. From New Orleans the empty barges will be pushed back upriver, either to St. Louis or Minneapolis/St. Paul, where they will be loaded with more cargo and assembled into tows. Then the trip downriver will begin all over again.

GLOSSARY

captain—the person in charge of a boat

cargo—anything that makes up the load carried by barges, trains, trucks, airplanes, ships, or other vehicles

chief engineer—the person in charge of all the mechanical workings on a boat

crew—all the people working under the captain on a towboat

current—In a river, water flows at different speeds. Where it is flowing fast, we say the current is strong.

dam—a large wall that blocks the flow of a body of water

dinner-bucket boat—a small towboat used to push barges from one place to another

downstream—the direction in which the river is flowing

export—to send something to another country

fuel efficiency—how well fuel is used by an engine. A car that gets 40 miles per gallon of gasoline has better fuel efficiency than a car that gets 30 miles per gallon.

galley—the kitchen on board a boat

lock—the passageway through a dam in which boats are raised or lowered from one water level to another

lower river—the Mississippi River between St. Louis, Missouri, and New Orleans, Louisiana

pilot—a person who is trained to steer a ship or a boat

tow—a group of barges fastened together

towboat—a boat used to push a tow of barges

upper river—the Mississippi River between Minneapolis/St. Paul, Minnesota, and St. Louis, Missouri

upstream—the direction opposite to that in which the river is flowing

valve—a mechanical device in a lock that opens in order to allow water to flow into or out of the lock

water level—the level at which a body of water sits when the water is still

In loving memory of Eggie and Lorne, who gave us so many treasured memories for keeps —M.M.S.

In loving memory of John Frederick Anthony —P.B.

Text copyright © 2016 by Mary McKenna Siddals
Jacket art and interior illustrations copyright © 2016 by Patrice Barton

Visit us on the Web! randomhousekids.com

Educators and librarians, for a variety of teaching tools, visit us at RHTeachersLibrarians.com

Library of Congress Cataloging-in-Publication Data
Siddals, Mary McKenna.
Bringing the outside in / by Mary McKenna Siddals ; illustrated by Patrice Barton. — First edition.
pages cm
Summary: A rhyming story that encourages children to get outside and play.
ISBN 978-0-449-81430-7 (hc) — ISBN 978-0-375-97165-5 (glb) — ISBN 978-0-375-98148-7 (ebk)
[1. Stories in rhyme. 2. Outdoor recreation—Fiction. 3. Play—Fiction.] I. Barton, Patrice, illustrator. II. Title.
PZ8.3.S5715Br 2016
[E]—dc23
2014048159

The illustrations in this book are pencil sketches colored digitally.

MANUFACTURED IN CHINA

10 9 8 7 6 5 4 3 2 1

First Edition

Random House Children's Books supports the First Amendment and celebrates the right to read.

Bringing the Outside In

By Mary McKenna Siddals

Illustrated by Patrice Barton

Random House 🏠 New York

We're bringing the outside in, oh,
Bringing the outside in . . .

Worms in our clutches,
Wind in our hair,
Boots full of puddle,
Mud everywhere!

Bringing the outside in, then . . .

Wiping it off,
Mopping it up,
Dumping it
out again.

We're bringing the outside in, oh,
Bringing the outside in . . .

Sea in our towels,
Shells in our pails,
Sun on our shoulders,
Sand in our tails!

Bringing the outside in, then . . .

Shaking it off,
Washing it up,
Drying it out again.

We're bringing the outside in, oh,
Bringing the outside in . . .

Bushels of apples,
Leaves stuck on clothes,
Acorns in pockets,
Smells in our nose!

Bringing the outside in, then . . .

Picking it off,
Sweeping it up,

Tossing it out again.

We're bringing the outside in, oh,
Bringing the outside in . . .

Snow in our collars,
Slush on our seats,
Nip in our fingers,
Icicle treats!

Bringing the outside in, then . . .

Brushing it off,
Warming it up,
Thawing it out again.

We're keeping the outside in, oh,
Keeping the outside in . . .

Treasures collected,
Pictures in heaps,
Stories remembered,
Memories for keeps!

Keeping the outside in, then . . .

Digging it up,
Dusting it off,
Bringing it out again, oh,

Bringing it out again!